Samsung Galaxy S25 Ultra User Guide for Seniors

The Complete 2025 Manual with Step-by-Step Tutorials, Hidden Features, and Smart Tips

By

Caleb R. Jennings

SAMSUNG GALAXY S25
ULTRA USER GUIDE
FOR SENIORS

The Complete 2025 Manual with Step-by-Step
Tutorials, Hidden Features, and Smart Tips

Caleb R. Jennings

Copyright © 2025 Caleb R. Jennings

Disclaimer

Table of Contents

Introduction

Understanding the Purpose of This Guide

The goal of this guide is to make using your Samsung Galaxy S25 Ultra an easy, enjoyable, and stress-free experience. Whether you've just purchased the phone or are trying to get more comfortable with using modern technology, this book is designed to walk you through everything—from the basics to advanced features—in a calm, patient, and easy-to-follow manner.

You do not need to be tech-savvy or have prior experience with smartphones to understand and benefit from this guide. Everything is explained step by step, in plain language, with helpful examples and tips designed for seniors and beginners alike.

This guide is more than just a manual—it's your assistant to help you confidently explore, communicate, and get the most out of your Samsung Galaxy S25 Ultra.

Who This Book is For

This book was created with seniors and first-time smartphone users in mind. If you've ever felt overwhelmed by new technology or hesitant to tap on something in fear of "messing it up," this book is for you.

It's also ideal for:

- Older adults transitioning from basic phones or older models
- Caregivers helping loved ones learn new devices
- Anyone who wants a slow-paced, straightforward approach to learning
- Users who prefer written instructions over video tutorials

If that sounds like you, rest assured—you're in the right place. You'll learn how to make calls, send messages, use the internet, take photos, adjust settings, and even explore smart features like voice assistants and hidden shortcuts—all with confidence.

What Makes the Samsung Galaxy S25 Ultra Unique

The Samsung Galaxy S25 Ultra is one of the most advanced smartphones released in 2025, and it combines powerful hardware with smart software. But what makes it special isn't just how advanced it is—it's how customizable and accessible it can be for users of all experience levels.

Some standout features include:

- A large, high-resolution display that's easy on the eyes
- A long-lasting battery for all-day use
- A professional-grade camera system for capturing clear, vibrant memories
- Android 15 and One UI 7, offering a clean, senior-friendly interface
- Accessibility tools like text magnification, voice commands, and simple modes

It's a device that can do a lot—but that doesn't mean learning it has to be difficult. This guide is here to show you how to use it in ways that matter most to you.

How to Navigate This Manual with Ease

This guide is structured in a way that lets you move at your own pace. You can read it from beginning to end, or jump to specific chapters depending on what you need help with. Each chapter is broken down into smaller sections that focus on individual tasks or features.

Here's how to make the most of it:

- Read one section at a time and follow along with your phone in hand
- Try out the examples and practice steps as you go
- Use the Appendix for quick definitions and shortcut references
- Return to sections anytime you want a refresher

There's no rush or pressure—just take your time and enjoy the learning journey.

A Simple Look at Android 15 and One UI 7

Your Galaxy S25 Ultra runs on Android 15, the latest version of Google's mobile operating system, and One UI 7, Samsung's custom user interface that sits on top of Android. They provide the software that powers your phone's features and settings.

In simple terms:

- **Android 15** controls the basic functions of your smartphone—like notifications, apps, security, and system updates.
- **One UI 7** makes everything look neat and user-friendly. It includes helpful design improvements, larger buttons, easier-to-read text, and intuitive navigation.

For seniors, this combination means your phone is more approachable than ever. Whether it's enlarging text, setting up voice commands, or simplifying your home screen, the system is built to help—not confuse—you.

Throughout this guide, you'll learn how to take advantage of these software features without needing technical knowledge. You'll discover how easy it can be to personalize your phone to suit your lifestyle and preferences.

Chapter One

Getting Started with Your Samsung Galaxy S25 Ultra

What's Inside the Box

When you open your Samsung Galaxy S25 Ultra box for the first time, you'll find several essential items neatly packed inside. Here's a quick list of what to expect:

- **Samsung Galaxy S25 Ultra smartphone**
- **USB-C charging cable**
- **Fast wall adapter (charging brick)**
- **SIM card ejector tool**
- **Quick Start Guide**
- **Warranty card and safety information**

Please note: Many modern phones no longer include earphones or a protective case in the box. If you need these, they can be purchased separately at a store or online.

Exploring the Physical Layout: Buttons, Ports, and Features

Before diving into using the phone, let's familiarize ourselves with its physical design.

Front Side:

- **Display screen** – The large touch screen is where most of your interaction takes place.
- **Front camera** – Located at the top center (used for selfies and video calls).

Back Side:

- **Rear cameras** – Multiple lenses for high-quality photos and videos.
- **Flash** – Helps in low-light photography.

Side Edges:

- **Right side:**
  - **Power button** – Used to turn the phone on/off or lock the screen.
  - **Volume buttons** – To raise or lower sound levels.
- **Left side:**
  - Usually clean with no buttons, depending on your model.

Bottom Edge:

- **USB-C port** – Where you plug in your charger or transfer data.
- **Speaker** – For audio output.
- **Microphone** – Used during calls or voice recordings.

Top Edge:

- **SIM/microSD card tray** – A small slot for inserting your SIM and storage card.

Inserting the SIM Card and microSD Card

To use mobile calling, texting, or data, your phone needs a **SIM card**. You can also insert a **microSD card** if you want extra storage space.

Steps to insert them:

1. **Power off** the phone before inserting anything.
2. Use the **SIM ejector tool** (included in the box). Gently insert it into the small hole on top of the phone.
3. The **SIM/microSD tray** will pop out.
4. Place your **nano-SIM card** and **microSD card (optional)** into the tray carefully—metal side facing down.
5. Gently push the tray back into place.

Your phone will recognize the SIM card after being turned on again.

Charging the Device and Battery Care Tips

Your Galaxy S25 Ultra comes with fast-charging capabilities, allowing your phone to power up quickly.

To charge your phone:

1. Plug the **USB-C cable** into the phone's charging port (bottom center).
2. Connect the other end to the **power adapter**, then plug it into a wall outlet.
3. The battery icon on the screen will show it's charging.

Battery care tips:

- Use the original charger to avoid damage.
- Avoid letting your battery drop to 0% often—try recharging around 20–30%.
- Unplug once it's fully charged to preserve long-term battery health.
- Avoid extreme temperatures while charging.

Turning the Phone On and Off

Turning your phone on and off is easy.

To turn it on:

- Press and **hold the Power button** (on the right side) for a few seconds until you see the Samsung logo.

To turn it off:

- Press and **hold the Power button** and **Volume Down button** at the same time until the power menu appears.
- Tap **Power off** or **Restart**.

You can also turn off your phone through the quick settings panel:

- Swipe down from the top of the screen and tap the **Power icon** in the corner.

Using the Touchscreen: Basic Gestures for Seniors

The touchscreen is how you'll interact with nearly everything on your phone. Don't worry—it's easy to get the hang of it. Here are the most common gestures:

- **Tap:** Lightly touch the screen once to open apps or select items.
- **Swipe:** Slide your finger across the screen (left, right, up, or down) to scroll or move between pages.
- **Pinch to Zoom:** Use two fingers to pinch in (to zoom out) or spread out (to zoom in)—great for photos and text.
- **Press and Hold:** Touch an item and keep your finger down for a moment to reveal more options (such as moving apps).
- **Drag:** After holding, you can move items around the screen.

If you find the screen too sensitive or difficult to read, don't worry—we'll cover how to adjust those settings in a later chapter.

Chapter Two

Easy Setup for First-Time Users

Step-by-Step Setup Process

When you turn on your Samsung Galaxy S25 Ultra for the first time, it will guide you through the initial setup. This process prepares your phone for daily use and helps personalize it to suit your needs. Take your time with each step, and don't worry—your phone will walk you through it.

Here's what to expect:

1. **Welcome Screen:**
   Tap **Start** to begin the setup process.
2. **Insert SIM Card (if not already inserted):**
   If you haven't inserted your SIM card yet, you'll be prompted to do so. You can also skip this step and do it later.

3. **Connect to Wi-Fi:**

   Select your home Wi-Fi network from the list and enter the password to connect.

4. **Terms and Conditions:**

   Read through and accept Samsung's terms by tapping **Agree** or **Next**.

5. **Transfer Data (Optional):**

   If you're switching from another phone, you can transfer your contacts, photos, and apps using **Samsung Smart Switch**. If not, choose **Skip** to set up as a new phone.

6. **Sign in to Google:**

   Use your existing Gmail address or create a new one. This connects you to apps like Gmail, YouTube, and the Play Store.

7. **Set a Lock Screen:**

   You can choose to use a **PIN**, **pattern**, **password**, or **biometric option** like **fingerprint** or **face recognition**. If preferred, you can skip this step and set it up later in settings.

8. **Finish Setup:**

   Your phone will finalize the setup, and you'll soon see your **Home screen**, ready to use.

Connecting to Wi-Fi and Mobile Data

You'll need an internet connection to download apps, browse the web, and stay connected. There are two main ways to connect:

To Connect to Wi-Fi:

1. Swipe down from the top of the screen to open the Quick Settings panel.
2. Tap the **Wi-Fi icon** (it looks like a radar signal).
3. Choose your Wi-Fi network and enter the password if prompted.
4. Tap **Connect**. A checkmark will appear once connected.

To Use Mobile Data:

If you have a SIM card with a data plan:

1. Swipe down to access Quick Settings.

2. Tap the **Mobile Data icon** to turn it on (it may say **LTE** or **5G**).

3. Your phone will use mobile internet when Wi-Fi is unavailable.

Tip: If you're on a limited data plan, try to stay connected to Wi-Fi when possible to avoid extra charges.

Signing in or Creating a Google Account

A **Google Account** is your key to unlocking many of your phone's most useful features, such as email, apps, cloud backup, and security tools.

To Sign In:

1. During setup, you'll see the Google sign-in screen.

2. Enter your Gmail address and tap **Next**.

3. Type your password and tap **Next** again.

4. Follow any prompts to verify your identity.

To Create a New Account:

1. Tap **Create account** at the sign-in screen.
2. Enter your first and last name.
3. Choose a new Gmail address and password.
4. Follow the remaining steps to confirm and finish.

You can always add more accounts later by going to: **Settings** > **Accounts and Backup** > **Manage Accounts**

Setting Your Preferred Language, Date, and Time

Your phone allows you to choose a language and time zone that matches where you live and how you prefer to read.

To Adjust Language Settings:

1. Go to **Settings**.
2. Tap **General Management** > **Language**.
3. Tap **Add Language** if you want to use a new one.

4. Select the language and set it as default.

To Set Date and Time:

1. Go to **Settings**.
2. Tap **General Management > Date and Time**.
3. If needed, disable **Automatic Date and Time** to manually enter your details.
4. Choose your **Time Zone** and set the correct **Date and Time**.

Most people keep automatic settings turned on, so the phone adjusts the time automatically based on location.

Activating Accessibility Features (Text Size, High Contrast, Screen Reader, etc.)

Samsung includes powerful **Accessibility options** to make the phone easier for everyone to use, especially seniors.

Here's how to activate them:

1. Open **Settings**.
2. Scroll down and tap **Accessibility**.

Helpful Accessibility Options for Seniors:

- **Visibility Enhancements:**
  - **Font Size and Style** – Enlarge text for easier reading.
  - **High Contrast Themes** – Adds bold outlines and contrast for better visibility.
  - **Magnifier Window** – Allows zooming into any part of the screen.
- **Hearing Enhancements:**
  - **Live Transcribe** – Converts spoken words to text.
  - **Sound Notifications** – Alerts you to doorbells, alarms, or crying babies.
- **Interaction and Dexterity:**
  - **Assistant Menu** – Adds an on-screen menu for easy access to features.
  - **Touch and Hold Delay** – Adjusts how quickly your phone reacts to touch.
- **Screen Reader:**
  - **TalkBack** – Reads aloud what's on the screen for users with low vision.

○ You can enable or disable it easily in the Accessibility menu.

These features are designed to give you more comfort and confidence as you use your phone daily.

Chapter Three

Mastering the Home Screen

Understanding the Layout: Home Screen, App Drawer, and Navigation Bar

Your **Home screen** is the main area you see when you turn on your Samsung Galaxy S25 Ultra. Think of it as your phone's desktop—it holds your most-used apps, widgets (like a clock or weather), and shortcuts.

Key parts of the Home screen:

- **App Icons:** Small images that open apps when tapped.
- **Widgets:** Small panels that show real-time info like the time, weather, or calendar.
- **Dock (Bottom Row):** A fixed area at the bottom with your favorite apps (like Phone, Messages, or Camera). These stay visible on all Home screen pages.

App Drawer:

The **App Drawer** is where all your installed apps live.

To open it:

- Swipe **up** from the bottom of the Home screen.
- You'll see every app installed on your phone in alphabetical order.
- You can tap and hold any app to move it to your Home screen for easier access.

Navigation Bar:

At the very bottom of your screen, you'll find the **Navigation bar**, which helps you move around your phone.

It usually has:

- **Back button** – Takes you one step back.
- **Home button** – Takes you to the Home screen.
- **Recent apps button** – Shows apps you've recently used.

You can customize this bar or switch to **gesture navigation**, which we'll cover next.

Using Buttons vs. Gesture Navigation

Samsung gives you two ways to control your phone: **buttons** or **gestures**. You can use whichever feels more comfortable.

Button Navigation (recommended for beginners):

- **Back button (triangle):** Returns to the previous screen.
- **Home button (circle):** Takes you back to the Home screen.
- **Recent apps (square or three lines):** Opens a view of your recent apps.

To enable:

- Go to **Settings > Display > Navigation Bar**
- Choose **Buttons**

Gesture Navigation (for advanced users):

- **Swipe up from the bottom center** to go Home

- **Swipe up and hold** to open recent apps
- **Swipe from the left or right edge** to go back

To enable:

- Go to **Settings > Display > Navigation Bar**
- Choose **Swipe Gestures**

You can switch back anytime if the gestures feel too fast or confusing.

Adding, Moving, and Removing App Icons

You can personalize your Home screen by placing your most-used apps right where you want them.

To Add an App:

1. Swipe up to open the App Drawer.
2. Tap and hold the app you want.
3. Drag it to the Home screen and let go.

To Move an App:

1. Tap and hold the app icon on the Home screen.

2. Drag it to a new position.

3. Let go when it's where you want it.

To Remove an App from the Home Screen:

1. Tap and hold the app.

2. Tap **Remove** (this removes the icon from the Home screen, not the app itself).

3. The app will still be in the App Drawer.

Tip: If you want to uninstall the app completely, choose **Uninstall** instead.

Creating Folders and Organizing Apps

If your Home screen starts to feel crowded, you can group related apps into **folders**.

To Create a Folder:

1. Tap and hold an app icon.

2. Drag it on top of another app and let go.

3. A folder is created automatically.

4. Tap the folder to rename it (e.g., "Games," "Social," or "Tools").

To Add More Apps to the Folder:

- Drag additional app icons into the folder.

To Remove an App from a Folder:

- Open the folder, tap and hold the app, and then drag it out.

This helps keep your phone neat and easier to navigate.

Changing Wallpapers and Themes

Personalizing your phone with your favorite image or color theme can make it feel more enjoyable to use.

To Change the Wallpaper:

1. Tap and hold a blank area on the Home screen.
2. Tap **Wallpaper and Style**.
3. Choose from **My Wallpapers**, **Gallery**, or **Wallpaper Services**.
4. Tap **Set as wallpaper** to apply it to the Home screen, Lock screen, or both.

To Change the Theme:

1. Open the **Settings** app.
2. Tap **Themes** (you may need a Samsung account).
3. Browse and download free or paid themes.
4. Tap **Apply** to change the overall look and feel of icons, menus, and colors.

Tip: Try dark mode for a softer screen appearance, especially helpful at night.

Chapter Four

Using the Phone App and Contacts

Making and Receiving Calls

The **Phone app** is where you make and receive calls. It's usually found on your Home screen with a green icon shaped like a phone receiver.

To Make a Call:

1. Open the **Phone app**.
2. Tap the **Keypad** tab to dial a number manually.
3. Enter the number and tap the **green call button**.
4. To end the call, tap the **red hang-up button**.

To Call a Saved Contact:

1. Tap the **Contacts** tab inside the Phone app.
2. Scroll or search for the person's name.
3. Tap their name, then tap the **call icon**.

To Answer a Call:

- When your phone rings, you'll see a green **Answer** button and a red **Decline** button.
- **Swipe the green button up** to answer.
- **Swipe the red button up** to reject the call.

If your phone is locked, the same options appear on the locked screen.

Saving, Editing, and Deleting Contacts

Managing your contact list makes calling friends and family easier. You can save details like names, phone numbers, email addresses, and birthdays.

To Save a New Contact:

1. Open the **Phone app** or **Contacts** app.
2. Tap the + **Add Contact** or **Create** button.
3. Enter the person's name and phone number.
4. Add extra details if you want (email, notes, photo).
5. Tap **Save**.

To Edit a Contact:

1. Open the **Contacts app**.
2. Tap the contact you want to edit.
3. Tap **Edit** (a pencil icon).
4. Make your changes, then tap **Save**.

To Delete a Contact:

1. Open the contact you wish to remove.
2. Tap **More** (three dots in the corner).
3. Tap **Delete**, then confirm.

Tip: If your contacts are synced with Google, changes will automatically update across your devices.

Blocking Unwanted Numbers

If you receive spam calls or someone you don't want to hear from, you can block the number.

To Block a Number:

1. Open the **Phone app**.
2. Tap **Recents** to find the number.

3. Tap the number, then the **i (info)** icon.

4. Tap **Block** at the bottom of the screen.

5. Confirm by tapping **Block** again.

You won't receive calls or texts from that number after it's blocked. You can unblock the number later in the **Blocked Numbers** settings.

Using the Speakerphone and Volume Controls

During a call, you can use the speakerphone to hear more clearly or talk hands-free.

To Use Speakerphone:

- During a call, tap the **Speaker icon** on the call screen.
- The icon will light up when active, and you'll hear the call through the loudspeaker.
- Tap it again to turn off speakerphone.

Adjusting Volume During a Call:

- Use the **Volume buttons** (on the right side of the phone) to make the call louder or softer.
- A volume slider will appear on-screen, showing the current level.

Tip: You can also plug in earphones or connect a Bluetooth device for private listening.

Understanding Voicemail and Call Settings

Voicemail allows callers to leave you a message when you're unavailable.

To Set Up Voicemail:

1. Open the **Phone app**.
2. Tap the **Keypad**, then press and hold **1**.
3. Follow the voice prompts to create a password and greeting.
4. When setup is complete, you'll be able to listen to messages by pressing **1** again.

Some carriers offer **Visual Voicemail**, where you can read and play messages from your screen without dialing.

To Access Call Settings:

1. Open the **Phone app**.
2. Tap the **three dots** in the top-right corner.
3. Tap **Settings**.

From here, you can:

- Manage blocked numbers
- Set up call forwarding
- Turn on caller ID and spam protection
- Change how your phone handles missed calls

These settings help customize how your calls work and keep you in control of your communication experience.

Chapter Five

Sending Messages and Emails

Sending and Receiving Text Messages (SMS & MMS)

Your Samsung Galaxy S25 Ultra makes texting easy and convenient. You can send simple text messages (**SMS**) or multimedia messages (**MMS**) that include pictures, videos, or voice clips.

To Send a Text Message:

1. Open the **Messages app** (usually found on your Home screen).
2. Tap the + **(compose)** button or **Start chat**.
3. Enter a contact name or phone number.
4. Tap the **message box** at the bottom and type your message.
5. Tap the **send icon** (paper airplane) to send it.

To Read and Reply to a Message:

- New messages will appear as notifications.
- Tap the message notification to open it.
- Tap the reply box to type and send a response.

Messages are grouped by contact, so your conversations are easy to follow.

Attaching Photos, Emojis, and Voice Notes

You can personalize your messages with photos, emojis, or even your voice.

To Attach a Photo:

1. Inside a message thread, tap the **paperclip or + icon**.
2. Choose **Gallery** to select a photo from your phone.
3. Tap the photo, then **Send**.

To Use Emojis:

- Tap the **smiley face icon** on the keyboard.
- Browse and tap an emoji to add it to your message.

To Send a Voice Note:

1. Tap the **microphone icon** in the message app.
2. Hold it down while speaking.
3. Release the button to send your voice message.

These features make texting more expressive and engaging, especially for staying connected with family and friends.

Using Samsung Messages vs. Google Messages

Your phone may come with both Samsung Messages and Google Messages. You can choose whichever feels easier to use.

Samsung Messages:

- Pre-installed on all Galaxy phones
- Simple, clean interface
- Works well with Samsung apps and features
- Supports chat features (if available from your carrier)

Google Messages:

- Available on the Play Store or pre-installed
- Offers better spam filtering and RCS chat features
- Can sync with your Google Account
- Great if you use other Google apps like Gmail and Calendar

How to Set Your Default Messaging App:

1. Go to **Settings > Apps > Choose default apps**
2. Tap **SMS app**
3. Select either **Samsung Messages** or **Google Messages**

You can switch at any time if you want to try the other.

Setting Up and Using Email (Gmail, Outlook, etc.)

Emails allow you to send messages, documents, and photos using your email address. The **Gmail app** is most commonly used on Android phones.

To Set Up an Email Account:

1. Open the **Gmail app** (or **Email app**).
2. Tap **Add account** if it doesn't open automatically.
3. Choose your provider (Gmail, Outlook, Yahoo, or Other).
4. Enter your email address and password.
5. Follow any security steps if prompted.

Once connected, you'll be able to send and receive emails immediately.

To Send an Email:

1. Open the Gmail app.
2. Tap the **Compose** button (bottom right).

3. Enter the recipient's email address.

4. Add a subject and write your message.

5. Tap the **Send** arrow.

You can also attach files and photos, just like in text messages.

Organizing and Managing Email Folders

Keeping your inbox organized makes it easier to find important emails.

Common Folders:

- **Inbox** – Where all new emails arrive
- **Sent** – Emails you've sent
- **Drafts** – Unfinished messages you saved
- **Spam** – Emails filtered as unwanted
- **Trash** – Recently deleted emails

To Move an Email to a Folder:

1. Open the email.

2. Tap the **three dots** (top right) or **Move to** icon.

3. Select the folder you want.

To Delete or Archive Emails:

- Swipe **left or right** on a message to archive or delete, depending on your settings.
- Tap and hold a message to select multiple emails, then tap the **trash can icon** to delete.

Tip: Check your Spam folder regularly in case important emails are sent there by mistake.

Chapter Six

Internet and Web Browsing

Connecting to the Internet via Wi-Fi or Data

To browse the internet, check email, or use most apps, your phone needs to be connected to the internet. You can connect either through **Wi-Fi** or your mobile provider's **data network**.

Connecting to Wi-Fi:

1. Swipe down from the top of the screen to open the **Quick Settings** menu.
2. Tap the **Wi-Fi icon** to turn it on.
3. Press and hold the icon to open the full Wi-Fi settings.
4. Tap the name of your home network.
5. Enter your **Wi-Fi password** and tap **Connect**.

Once connected, your phone will remember this
network and reconnect automatically.

Using Mobile Data:

If you have a SIM card with a data plan:

1. Swipe down and tap the **Mobile Data icon**
   (shows LTE or 5G when active).
2. Your phone will use your carrier's data
   connection when Wi-Fi is not available.

Tip: Use Wi-Fi whenever possible to reduce data
charges, especially if you have a limited mobile plan.

Using the Samsung Internet and Chrome Browsers

Your Galaxy S25 Ultra comes with two main browsers:
Samsung Internet and Google Chrome. Both work well
for viewing websites and searching online.

Opening a Browser:

1. Tap the **Samsung Internet** or **Chrome** icon from the Home screen or App Drawer.
2. At the top, you'll see a search or address bar.
3. Type in a website (e.g., www.weather.com) or search term (e.g., "local news").
4. Tap **Go** or the magnifying glass icon to begin browsing.

Both browsers offer features like tabbed browsing, bookmarks, and privacy controls. You can use whichever one feels more comfortable.

Differences at a Glance:

- **Samsung Internet:** Simple, senior-friendly layout with built-in privacy settings.
- **Chrome:** Syncs easily with your Google account and bookmarks across devices.

You can set either browser as your default in **Settings > Apps > Choose default apps > Browser app**.

Bookmarking Favorite Websites

Bookmarks make it easy to return to your favorite websites with one tap—just like saving a shortcut.

To Bookmark a Website:

1. While visiting the site, tap the **menu icon** (three lines or dots).
2. Tap **Add to Bookmarks** (Samsung) or **Star icon** (Chrome).
3. The site will be saved in your Bookmarks list.

To Access Bookmarks Later:

- In **Samsung Internet**, tap the **Bookmarks icon** (shaped like a star).
- In **Chrome**, tap the **three-dot menu**, then select **Bookmarks**.

You can rename or delete bookmarks at any time by opening the bookmark list and tapping **Edit** or **More options**.

Using Reader Mode and Zoom Options

Some websites can be hard to read, especially if they're cluttered or use small text. That's where **Reader Mode** and **Zoom** features can help.

Reader Mode (Samsung Internet only):

1. Open a website with a long article or news story.
2. Tap the **Reader Mode icon** (usually at the top of the screen; it looks like a page).
3. The page will be reformatted to a clean, easy-to-read layout without ads or pop-ups.

You can change the font size, background color, and text style for more comfort.

Zooming In and Out:

- Use **two fingers** on the screen:
  - Spread fingers apart to **zoom in**.
  - Pinch fingers together to **zoom out**.
- You can also adjust text size in **Settings > Accessibility > Visibility enhancements > Font size and style**.

Zooming is especially helpful when reading news, shopping online, or viewing photos.

Internet Safety Tips for Seniors

The internet is a valuable tool, but it's important to stay safe while using it. Here are some essential safety tips to keep in mind:

Avoid Suspicious Links:

- Do not click on links in emails or messages from people you don't know.
- Be cautious of websites that ask for personal or financial information.

Use Secure Websites:

- Look for **https://** at the beginning of a website's address—it means the site is secure.
- A small **lock icon** in the address bar is another good sign.

Keep Your Phone Updated:

- Regular updates help fix security issues.
- Go to **Settings > Software update > Download and install** to check for updates.

Avoid Sharing Personal Information:

- Never share your Social Security number, bank details, or passwords online unless you're sure the site is legitimate.

Use Strong Passwords:

- Use a mix of letters, numbers, and symbols.
- Don't use the same password for all your accounts.

By following these tips, you can enjoy browsing the web with confidence and peace of mind.

Chapter Seven

Taking and Viewing Photos and Videos

Opening and Using the Camera App

Your Samsung Galaxy S25 Ultra has one of the most powerful camera systems available on a smartphone. It allows you to take high-quality photos and videos effortlessly.

To Open the Camera:

- Tap the **Camera icon** on your Home screen or App Drawer.
- Or, **double-press the Power button** quickly to launch the camera from any screen (even when the phone is locked).

Once open, you'll see a live view of what the camera sees. The shutter buttons and mode options will appear at the bottom.

Basic Camera Layout:

- **Shutter button (white circle):** Tap to take a photo.
- **Video button (red circle):** Tap to start recording video.
- **Switch camera icon:** Tap to switch between front (selfie) and rear camera.
- **Gallery preview (small image):** Tap to view your most recent photo or video.

Taking Photos and Recording Videos

Taking a picture or recording a video is as easy as pointing your camera and tapping a button.

To Take a Photo:

1. Open the **Camera app**.
2. Point your phone at your subject.

3. Tap the **white shutter button** to capture the photo.

The camera focuses automatically, but you can tap the screen to focus on a specific area.

To Record a Video:

1. Open the **Camera app**.
2. Tap the **Video tab** at the bottom.
3. Press the **red record button** to begin recording.
4. Tap the same button again to stop.

Videos are saved automatically to your phone's gallery.

Using Camera Modes (Portrait, Night, Zoom, etc.)

The Galaxy S25 Ultra includes multiple camera modes that let you get creative or improve your results in different lighting and conditions.

Portrait Mode (also called Live Focus):

- Blurs the background and keeps the subject sharp.
- Best for people, pets, or close-up objects.
- Swipe to **Portrait** mode and frame your subject.

Night Mode:

- Improves photo clarity in low-light situations.
- Swipe to **Night** mode, hold the phone steady, and tap the shutter.

Zoom:

- Tap or pinch the screen to zoom in or out.
- You can also tap the **zoom buttons** (like 3x or 10x) for preset zoom levels.

Pro Mode (Advanced Users):

- Lets you adjust focus, exposure, ISO, and other settings manually.

You can explore these modes by swiping left or right across the bottom of the camera screen.

Viewing, Editing, and Deleting Media

Once you've taken photos or videos, they're automatically saved in your **Gallery app** or **Google Photos**, depending on your settings.

To View Photos or Videos:

1. Open the **Gallery app**.
2. Tap **Pictures** or **Albums** to browse.
3. Tap any photo or video to view it full screen.

To Edit a Photo:

1. Open the photo in the Gallery.
2. Tap the **Edit icon** (pencil shape).
3. You can crop, rotate, adjust brightness, or apply filters.
4. Tap **Save** to apply the changes.

To Delete a Photo or Video:

1. Tap the photo to open it.
2. Tap the **trash can icon**.
3. Confirm by tapping **Move to Trash**.

Deleted items stay in the **Trash folder** for 30 days before being permanently removed.

Organizing Photos into Albums

Creating albums helps keep your photos sorted by event, subject, or purpose.

To Create an Album:

1. Open the **Gallery app**.
2. Tap the **Albums** tab.
3. Tap + **(Create album)**.
4. Enter a name (e.g., "Family Trip" or "Pets") and tap **Create**.
5. Select photos to move into the album by tapping and holding, then choosing **Move to album**.

This keeps your memories organized and easier to find later.

Sharing Photos via Text, Email, or Social Media

Sharing photos is a great way to stay connected with loved ones. Your phone makes it simple.

To Share a Photo:

1. Open the photo in the **Gallery**.
2. Tap the **Share icon** (three connected dots or triangle shape).
3. Choose how you want to share:
   - **Messages** – Send via text
   - **Email** – Send as an attachment
   - **WhatsApp, Facebook, or other apps** – If installed
4. Select the contact or enter the email/phone number.
5. Tap **Send** or **Post**.

You can also share multiple photos by selecting them first, then tapping **Share**.

Chapter Eight

Essential Apps for Daily Life

Weather, Calendar, Alarm, and Clock

Your Samsung Galaxy S25 Ultra comes with built-in apps to help you stay informed, organized, and on schedule.

Weather App:

- Shows real-time local weather, forecasts, and alerts.
- Open the **Weather app** from your Home screen or swipe right on the main screen (Samsung Free).
- You can also add a weather **widget** to your Home screen for quick updates.

Calendar App:

- Lets you schedule events, set reminders, and view holidays.
- Open the **Calendar app**, tap + **(Add)** to create an event.
- You can set the date, time, repeat options, and even receive alerts.

Alarm & Clock App:

- Found under the **Clock app**.
- Use it to set alarms, timers, check world clocks, or use the stopwatch.
- To set an alarm:
  1. Open **Clock** > tap **Alarm** > tap +
  2. Set the time and days you want it to repeat
  3. Tap **Save**

This is great for waking up, remembering to take medication, or staying on track throughout the day.

Using the Calculator and Notes

These tools are simple but incredibly useful for everyday tasks.

Calculator App:

- Open the **Calculator** from your Apps screen.
- Use it for basic calculations or rotate your phone horizontally for more advanced functions.
- You can copy/paste numbers and view calculation history with the **History** icon.

Samsung Notes:

- Helps you jot down shopping lists, reminders, or quick ideas.
- Open the **Samsung Notes** app and tap the + to create a new note.
- You can type, draw, or use voice dictation.
- Notes are automatically saved and can be organized into folders.

Downloading and Updating Apps from the Play Store

The **Google Play Store** is your gateway to thousands of apps—many free—that can improve your daily life.

To Download an App:

1. Open the **Play Store** from your Home screen.
2. Tap the **Search bar** at the top and type the app's name (e.g., "Zoom" or "Bible").
3. Tap the correct app from the results.
4. Tap **Install**. The app will download and appear on your Home screen.

To Update Apps:

1. Open the **Play Store**.
2. Tap your **profile icon** in the top-right corner.
3. Tap **Manage apps & device**.
4. Tap **Update All** to keep all your apps current.

Keeping apps updated improves performance and security.

Using Google Maps and GPS Navigation

Google Maps is one of the most powerful tools on your Galaxy S25 Ultra. It helps you find directions, avoid traffic, and locate businesses or landmarks.

To Get Directions:

1. Open the **Google Maps** app.
2. Tap the **Search bar** and enter your destination (e.g., "pharmacy" or "123 Main Street").
3. Tap **Directions**.
4. Choose a mode of travel (car, walk, public transit).
5. Tap **Start** to begin voice-guided navigation.

Extra Features:

- Tap **Explore** to see nearby restaurants, gas stations, or attractions.
- Save **Home** and **Work** locations for one-tap directions.

Google Maps uses voice prompts, so you don't have to look at your phone while driving.

Health and Wellness Apps for Seniors

Your phone can support your well-being through health tracking and lifestyle apps. Here are a few useful ones:

Samsung Health:

- Pre-installed on your phone.
- Tracks steps, heart rate (with compatible devices), sleep, and water intake.
- You can set daily goals and log your progress.

Pill Reminder & Medication Tracker:

- Available in the Play Store.
- Helps remind you when to take medication.
- Sends notifications and tracks dosage history.

Simple Relaxation & Fitness Apps:

- **Calm** or **Headspace** for meditation and sleep support.
- **Senior Fitness Workouts** – Gentle exercise routines designed for older adults.

- **Stretching and Balance apps** – Improve flexibility and mobility.

Always check app reviews and permissions before installing. Many health apps are free, with optional upgrades.

Chapter Nine

Staying Connected with Family and Friends

Using WhatsApp, Facebook, and Other Social Apps

Your Samsung Galaxy S25 Ultra gives you several ways to stay in touch with loved ones—whether it's through messages, pictures, or video calls.

WhatsApp:

- A free app for messaging, calling, and video chatting over Wi-Fi or mobile data.
- To get started:
    1. Download WhatsApp from the **Play Store**.
    2. Open the app and follow the setup prompts (enter your phone number and name).

3. Tap the **chat icon** to message or call saved contacts who also use WhatsApp.

Facebook:

- A social platform to share updates, view family photos, and connect with friends.
- To use it:
  1. Download the **Facebook app** from the Play Store.
  2. Sign in or create an account.
  3. Use the **News Feed** to scroll updates or **Messenger** to chat privately.

Other Popular Apps:

- **Instagram:** Share and view photos.
- **Messenger:** Facebook's separate app for private conversations.
- **Nextdoor or Telegram:** Local and group messaging communities.

Tip: All social apps can be resized and organized on your Home screen for easier access.

Video Calling with Google Meet or Zoom

Seeing the faces of loved ones makes conversations more meaningful. You can make video calls using **Google Meet** or **Zoom**.

Using Google Meet:

1. Open the **Google Meet** app (usually pre-installed).
2. Tap **New Meeting** or **Join with a code**.
3. Share the link with others or enter the code they gave you.
4. Tap **Join** to start the call.

Google Meet works well with Gmail and Calendar, making it ideal for scheduled family chats.

Using Zoom:

1. Download **Zoom** from the Play Store.
2. Sign in or join as a guest.
3. Tap **Join a Meeting** and enter the meeting ID.
4. Tap **Join** to enter the call.

Zoom includes options like muting, turning off video, or chatting during calls.

Setting Up Emergency Contacts

Your phone allows you to save **emergency contacts** that first responders can access—even if the phone is locked.

To Add Emergency Contacts:

1. Open the **Contacts** app.
2. Tap your own name (your profile).
3. Scroll down to find **Emergency contacts**.
4. Tap **Add** and choose trusted contacts (family, friends, caregiver).

These contacts can be reached from your lock screen in case of an emergency.

Using the SOS and Emergency Features

The Galaxy S25 Ultra has built-in safety tools to help you call for help quickly.

To Enable SOS Messages:

1. Go to **Settings > Safety and emergency > Send SOS messages**.
2. Turn it on.
3. Choose up to four emergency contacts.
4. You can enable the option to attach photos and audio when the alert is sent.

To Trigger SOS:

- **Quickly press the Power button 3 to 5 times** in a row.
- Your phone will automatically send a message with your location to your emergency contacts.

Other Emergency Features:

- **Medical Info:** Add your allergies, medications, and blood type in the **Medical Info** section under **Safety and emergency**.
- **Emergency Alert Sound:** Set your phone to play a loud alarm when activated.

These tools offer peace of mind and are especially helpful when living alone or in case of sudden emergencies.

Managing Notifications and Alerts

Staying updated is important, but too many notifications can become overwhelming. You can easily control which apps send alerts and how often.

To View Notifications:

- Swipe down from the top of the screen to see new messages, emails, and alerts.
- Tap a notification to open it or swipe it left/right to dismiss it.

To Manage Notification Settings:

1. Go to **Settings > Notifications**.
2. Tap **App notifications**.
3. Turn notifications **on or off** for individual apps.

Customize Notification Style:

- Choose **Brief** (simplified) or **Detailed** (shows more info).
- Go to **Settings** > **Notifications** > **Notification pop-up style** to select your preference.

Tip: You can also set "Do Not Disturb" hours to silence all alerts temporarily—useful at night or during rest periods.

Chapter Ten

Customizing Your Phone Experience

Adjusting Display Settings (Brightness, Font, Screen Timeout)

Your Galaxy S25 Ultra offers several ways to make the screen easier on your eyes and more comfortable to use. You can adjust the brightness, font size, and how long the screen stays on when inactive.

To Change Screen Brightness:

1. Swipe down from the top of the screen to open the Quick Settings panel.
2. Use the **brightness slider** to increase or decrease screen brightness.

To Adjust Font Size:

1. Open **Settings**.
2. Tap **Display > Font size and style**.
3. Use the slider to make the text larger or smaller.
4. You can also change the font style for a more personalized look.

To Set Screen Timeout:

1. Go to **Settings > Display > Screen timeout**.
2. Choose how long the screen stays on when not in use (e.g., 30 seconds, 2 minutes).

Longer timeouts are helpful if you read slowly; shorter timeouts save battery.

Changing Ringtones and Notification Sounds

You can assign a ringtone that suits your taste and helps you recognize calls and messages easily.

To Change Your Ringtone:

1. Open **Settings**.

2. Tap **Sounds and vibration > Ringtone**.

3. Tap to preview the available tones.

4. Select the one you like and tap **Back** to save it.

To Set Notification Sounds:

1. Go to **Settings > Sounds and vibration > Notification sound**.

2. Choose a tone from the list.

3. You can set different tones for different apps, like Messages and Email.

Tip: You can also download custom ringtones or use music clips from your phone.

Setting Do Not Disturb and Bedtime Mode

When you want quiet time—like during sleep or meetings—you can use **Do Not Disturb** and **Bedtime Mode** to limit interruptions.

To Turn On Do Not Disturb:

1. Open **Settings** > **Notifications** > **Do Not Disturb**.
2. Toggle it on or set a **schedule** (for example, from 10:00 PM to 7:00 AM).
3. You can allow exceptions for specific people or alarms.

To Use Bedtime Mode:

1. Go to **Settings** > **Modes and Routines** > **Bedtime mode**.
2. Schedule the time for Bedtime Mode to activate.
3. The screen dims, switches to grayscale, and silences nonessential sounds.

Both features help you sleep better and reduce stress by minimizing late-night alerts.

Customizing the Lock Screen and Always-On Display

The **Lock screen** appears when your phone is turned on but not yet unlocked. You can personalize it with a message, clock style, or photo.

To Customize the Lock Screen:

1. Open **Settings > Lock screen**.
2. Choose from options like:
   - **Clock style** – Change the look and placement.
   - **Contact info** – Add your name or emergency message.
   - **Wallpaper** – Set a different image than the Home screen.

Always-On Display:

This feature shows the time, date, and battery even when the phone is locked.

To enable or customize:

1. Go to **Settings** > **Lock screen** > **Always On Display**.
2. Turn it on and select your preferred style and schedule.

It helps you check the time without touching your phone.

Using the Edge Panel for Quick Access

The **Edge Panel** is a convenient tool that gives you quick access to your favorite apps, contacts, and tools.

To Enable Edge Panel:

1. Open **Settings** > **Display** > **Edge Panels**.
2. Turn on **Edge Panels**.
3. Tap **Panels** to choose what appears (apps, weather, clipboard, etc.).

To Use It:

- Look for a **small handle** on the right or left side of your screen.
- Swipe it inward to open the Edge Panel.

- Tap an app or tool to use it instantly.

You can reposition or resize the Edge Panel handle to suit your comfort.

Chapter Eleven

Exploring Hidden Features and Smart Tools

Using Bixby and Google Assistant

Your Galaxy S25 Ultra includes two built-in voice assistants: Bixby (Samsung's assistant) and Google Assistant. Both can help you complete tasks using your voice—great for hands-free use.

Using Google Assistant:

Google Assistant is helpful for asking questions, setting reminders, sending texts, or opening apps.

To activate:

- Say **"Hey Google"** or **"OK Google"**, or
- Press and hold the **Home button** (if using gesture navigation, swipe from the bottom corner).

Examples of what you can say:

- "What's the weather today?"
- "Send a text to Sarah."
- "Remind me to take medicine at 9 AM."
- "Call John."

To enable or adjust Google Assistant settings:

- Go to **Settings > Google > Settings for Google apps > Search, Assistant & Voice**.

Using Bixby:

Bixby can control your phone's settings and respond to commands, such as adjusting brightness or taking a screenshot.

To use Bixby:

- Press and hold the **Side key** (Power button) if assigned to Bixby.
- Or open the **Bixby app**.

You can ask Bixby to:

- "Turn on Bluetooth."
- "Set a timer for 10 minutes."
- "Open the Camera."

If you prefer one voice assistant over the other, you can disable the one you don't use in Settings.

Samsung Smart Switch for Transferring Data

Smart Switch helps you move data (photos, messages, contacts, apps) from your old phone to your new Galaxy S25 Ultra—whether your previous device was Android or iPhone.

To Use Smart Switch:

1. Open the **Smart Switch app** (pre-installed).
2. Choose how to transfer:
    - **Wireless** (recommended for Android phones)
    - **Cable** connection (recommended for iPhones)
3. Follow the prompts on both phones.

4. Choose what data to move (contacts, messages, photos, etc.).

5. Wait for the transfer to complete.

It's an easy, secure way to keep all your important content when upgrading to a new phone.

Multi-Window and Split-Screen Mode

You can use **two apps at once** with Multi-Window—perfect for multitasking, like watching a video while texting or browsing the web while checking email.

To Use Split-Screen:

1. Tap the **Recent Apps** button (or swipe up and hold from the bottom if using gestures).
2. Tap the **app icon** at the top of the preview.
3. Tap **Open in split screen view**.
4. Choose the second app to display on the bottom half of the screen.

You can drag the divider to resize the windows or swipe it down to close split view.

This feature helps you stay productive without constantly switching between apps.

Digital Wellbeing and Screen Time Monitoring

Digital Wellbeing is a built-in tool that helps you monitor how much time you spend on your phone and encourages healthy usage habits.

To Access Digital Wellbeing:

1. Open **Settings > Digital Wellbeing and parental controls**.
2. See a **dashboard** showing screen time, app usage, and unlocks.
3. Tap each section for detailed insights.

Features You Can Use:

- **App timers** – Set daily time limits on specific apps.
- **Focus Mode** – Pause distracting apps temporarily.

- **Bedtime Mode** – Dims your screen and silences calls at night.

This is a great tool for setting boundaries and avoiding screen fatigue.

Hidden Camera and Gallery Tricks

Your camera and gallery apps include a few clever features that make photo-taking and organizing more enjoyable.

Camera Shortcuts:

- **Quick launch**: Double-press the **Power button** to open the Camera instantly.
- **Palm shutter**: Hold your hand up to the camera to take a photo automatically—great for selfies without touching the screen.
  - Enable this in **Camera Settings > Shooting methods**.

Gallery Tricks:

- **Favorite photos**: Tap the **heart icon** on a photo to mark it as a favorite—it's then saved to a separate "Favorites" album.

- **Search by keyword**: Use the search bar in the Gallery to find photos by location, people, or objects (e.g., "beach," "birthday").

- **Revert edits**: If you change a photo and don't like the result, open it again, tap **Edit > Revert**, and your original version returns.

These small tools make organizing and enjoying your photos easier and more fun.

Chapter Twelve

Troubleshooting and Maintenance

Common Problems and How to Fix Them

Even the best smartphones can run into occasional problems. Fortunately, most issues are easy to fix without needing technical knowledge.

Phone Feels Slow or Freezes:

- **What to try:**
    1. Close unused apps running in the background.
    2. Restart your phone.
    3. Clear unnecessary files (covered later in this chapter).

Battery Drains Too Quickly:

- **What to check:**
    1. Lower screen brightness.

2. Close apps not in use.

3. Check for battery-hungry apps under **Settings > Battery and device care > Battery usage**.

Wi-Fi or Bluetooth Not Connecting:

- **Steps to fix:**
    1. Turn Wi-Fi or Bluetooth off and back on.
    2. Restart your phone.
    3. Reconnect to the network or device manually.

Apps Keep Crashing:

- **Fix by:**
    1. Updating the app in the Play Store.
    2. Clearing app cache under **Settings > Apps > [App Name] > Storage > Clear cache**.

These basic solutions solve most common issues and help keep your phone running smoothly.

Restarting, Resetting, and Safe Mode

When your phone misbehaves, restarting or resetting it can often solve the problem.

To Restart Your Phone:

1. Press and hold the **Power button and Volume Down button** together.
2. Tap **Restart** and wait for the device to reboot.

To Perform a Soft Reset (when screen is unresponsive):

- Press and hold **Power + Volume Down** for about 10 seconds until the phone restarts.

To Use Safe Mode:

Safe Mode lets you run your phone with only essential apps. This helps diagnose issues caused by third-party apps.

1. Press and hold the **Power button**.
2. Tap and hold **Power off** until you see **Safe mode**.
3. Tap **Safe mode** to restart the phone.

4. To exit, restart your phone normally.

To Reset Settings (without erasing data):

1. Go to **Settings** > **General management** > **Reset**.
2. Tap **Reset all settings**.

Only your settings will be reset—your photos, contacts, and apps will remain safe.

Managing Storage and Freeing Up Space

Over time, your phone can fill up with apps, photos, and downloads. Freeing up space helps it perform better.

To Check Storage:

1. Open **Settings** > **Battery and device care** > **Storage**.
2. View how much space is used by apps, photos, and files.

Tips to Free Up Space:

- Delete unused apps:

  Go to **Settings** > **Apps**, select the app, and tap **Uninstall**.

- Remove duplicate or blurry photos:

  Open **Gallery**, review albums, and delete unnecessary images.

- Clear Downloads:

  Open the **My Files** app, tap **Downloads**, and remove old files.

You can also use the **Device care** tool to automatically optimize storage and performance.

Updating Software and Apps

Software updates fix bugs, improve security, and add new features.

To Update Your Phone's Software:

1. Open **Settings** > **Software update** > **Download and install**.
2. If an update is available, tap **Install now**.

Your phone may restart after installation.

To Update Apps:

1. Open the **Play Store**.
2. Tap your **profile icon** in the top-right corner.
3. Tap **Manage apps & device** > **Updates available**.
4. Tap **Update all**.

Keeping your apps and phone updated ensures smooth and safe operation.

Keeping Your Phone Secure with Samsung Knox

Samsung Knox is a built-in security platform that protects your personal data from malware, viruses, and unauthorized access.

How Knox Protects You:

- Monitors system integrity and blocks harmful activity.

- Protects your passwords and biometric data (fingerprint, face recognition).
- Secures your files and personal information in real time.

Using Secure Folder:

Knox allows you to create a **Secure Folder** to store private photos, notes, and apps.

To Set It Up:

1. Go to **Settings > Security and privacy > Secure Folder**.
2. Sign in to your Samsung account.
3. Set up a lock method (PIN, fingerprint, etc.).
4. Move files or apps into the folder for extra protection.

With Samsung Knox, your information stays protected—even if your phone is lost or stolen.

Chapter Thirteen

Privacy, Safety, and Security

Setting Up Fingerprint and Face Recognition

The Galaxy S25 Ultra offers two convenient biometric security options—**fingerprint scanning** and **face recognition**—to help you unlock your phone quickly and securely.

To Set Up Fingerprint Recognition:

1. Open **Settings**.
2. Tap **Security and privacy** > **Biometrics** > **Fingerprints**.
3. Follow the prompts to scan your fingerprint (you may need to set a PIN or pattern first).
4. Place your finger on the sensor (under the screen) and lift it repeatedly as instructed.
5. Tap **Done** when finished.

You can add more than one fingerprint if desired.

To Set Up Face Recognition:

1. Go to **Settings** > **Security and privacy** > **Biometrics** > **Face recognition**.
2. Follow the on-screen steps to register your face.
3. Hold the phone at eye level and look at the screen.
4. Tap **Done** when complete.

Tip: These features add extra security without the need to remember passwords and can be used alongside your lock screen.

Creating a Secure Lock Screen

A secure lock screen prevents others from accessing your phone without permission. You can choose from several lock options:

- **PIN:** A 4-digit code.
- **Pattern:** A connect-the-dots shape.
- **Password:** A longer passcode with letters and numbers.

- **Biometrics:** Fingerprint or face unlock.

To Set Your Lock Method:

1. Open **Settings**.
2. Tap **Lock screen > Screen lock type**.
3. Select your preferred method and follow the setup instructions.

Always choose a code that's easy for you to remember but hard for others to guess. Avoid simple combinations like 1234 or your birth year.

Managing App Permissions

Apps often request permission to access parts of your phone, such as your camera, location, or contacts. While many apps are safe, it's important to know what access each one has.

To View and Adjust App Permissions:

1. Open **Settings > Security and privacy > Permission manager**.

2. Choose a category (e.g., Location, Microphone, Camera).

3. Tap each app to allow or deny access.

For example:

- You might want your map app to access your location,
- But a game app doesn't need it and can be denied.

Regularly checking permissions keeps your data more secure and prevents apps from using more than they need.

Using Find My Mobile if Your Phone is Lost

Samsung's **Find My Mobile** service helps you locate, lock, or erase your phone if it's ever lost or stolen.

To Set It Up:

1. Open **Settings > Security and privacy > Find My Mobile**.

2. Sign in with your **Samsung account**.

3. Turn on **Remote unlock** and **Send last location**.

To Use Find My Mobile:

1. Visit findmymobile.samsung.com from another device or computer.

2. Sign in with your Samsung account.

3. You can:
   - **Locate** your phone on a map
   - **Ring** it at full volume
   - **Lock** it remotely
   - **Erase** data if the phone can't be recovered

This tool gives you peace of mind knowing you can still protect your information even if the phone is out of reach.

Avoiding Scams, Pop-Ups, and Dangerous Apps

Staying safe online is essential, especially when browsing the internet or downloading apps.

Tips to Stay Safe:

- **Only use trusted apps:**

  Download from the **Google Play Store** only.
  Avoid installing apps from websites or
  unfamiliar links.

- **Watch for pop-up ads:**

  Never click on pop-ups that say your phone is
  infected or offer free prizes. These are scams.

- **Check app reviews and permissions:**

  Before downloading an app, read the reviews
  and see what permissions it requests.

- **Beware of suspicious emails or texts:**

  Do not open links or attachments from
  unknown senders. If a message seems strange, it
  probably is.

- **Install Google Play Protect:**

  This built-in feature scans apps for harmful
  behavior.

  To check:

  1. Open **Play Store**.
  2. Tap your profile icon > **Play Protect** >
     Scan.

These steps will help keep your phone, personal information, and finances safe.

Chapter Fourteen

Tips, Tricks, and Shortcuts

Time-Saving Gestures and Quick Settings

Your Galaxy S25 Ultra is designed to help you move faster and get more done with simple gestures and one-swipe access to important tools.

Useful Gestures:

- **Swipe Down (Twice) for Quick Settings:**
  Swipe down once from the top of the screen for notifications. Swipe down again for Quick Settings (Wi-Fi, Bluetooth, flashlight, etc.).
- **Swipe Up for App Drawer:**
  From the Home screen, swipe up to view all installed apps.
- **Double Tap to Wake or Sleep:**
  Go to **Settings > Advanced features >**

Motions and gestures to enable "Double tap to turn on/off screen."

- **Swipe from Left or Right to Go Back:** If using gesture navigation, swipe in from either side of the screen to return to the previous screen.

These gestures save time and reduce the need for multiple button presses.

Keyboard Tips for Easier Typing

Typing doesn't have to be frustrating. The Samsung keyboard includes helpful features to make it smoother and easier.

Tips to Try:

- **Voice Typing:** Tap the **microphone icon** on the keyboard to speak instead of type.
- **Emoji and Symbols:** Tap the **smiley face icon** for emojis, or hold the **period key (.)** to access symbols.

- **Predictive Text:**

  Turn on **predictive text** to get word suggestions as you type.

  Go to **Settings > General management > Samsung Keyboard settings > Predictive text**.

- **Enlarge the Keyboard:**

  You can increase keyboard size in **Keyboard settings > Size and transparency**.

These tools help reduce typing errors and make communication quicker and more comfortable.

Battery-Saving Tips for Longer Use

To keep your phone powered throughout the day, try these simple strategies:

Practical Tips:

- **Lower Screen Brightness:**

  Swipe down and adjust the **brightness slider** manually.

- **Enable Power Saving Mode:**

  Go to **Settings > Battery and device care >**
  Battery > Power saving and turn it on.

- **Use Dark Mode:**

  Dark backgrounds use less power.

  Find it under **Settings > Display > Dark**
  mode.

- **Close Unused Apps:**

  Tap the **Recent Apps** button and swipe away
  apps not currently in use.

- **Turn Off Features You Don't Need:**

  Turn off Wi-Fi, Bluetooth, or Location when
  not in use.

By following these tips, your battery will last longer and
your phone will run more efficiently.

Hidden Shortcuts You'll Love

The S25 Ultra includes hidden shortcuts that can
simplify tasks and reduce the number of steps needed to
get things done.

Quick Tips:

- **Swipe Edge Panel for Favorites:**
  Enable the **Edge Panel** to quickly access your most-used apps or contacts.
- **Pin App Pairs for Split-Screen:**
  Use **Multi-Window mode**, then tap the divider and select **Add app pair to Edge panel** for one-tap split-screen access later.
- **Back Tap (if available):**
  In some models, you can assign actions to double-tapping the back of the phone (found in **Labs** or **Advanced Features**, if supported).
- **Quick Launch Camera:**
  Double-press the **Power button** quickly to open the camera at any time.

These features may seem small, but they add up to big savings in time and effort.

Helpful Voice Commands to Simplify Your Life

Whether you're cooking, driving, or simply prefer speaking to typing, voice commands through **Google Assistant** or **Bixby** can make everyday tasks easier.

Examples of Google Assistant Commands:

- "What's on my calendar today?"
- "Send a text to Emily."
- "Set a timer for 20 minutes."
- "What's the weather in Chicago?"
- "Open YouTube."

Examples of Bixby Commands:

- "Turn on Wi-Fi."
- "Take a screenshot."
- "Read my messages."
- "Open Settings."
- "Call my daughter."

You can trigger Google Assistant by saying **"Hey Google"** or holding the **Home button**, and Bixby by pressing the **Side key** (if assigned).

Voice commands offer a helpful alternative to touching the screen—especially useful for multitasking or accessibility.

Conclusion

Keeping Your Phone Up to Date

One of the best ways to keep your Galaxy S25 Ultra running smoothly and securely is by staying up to date with the latest software and app updates.

Why Updates Matter:

- Improve performance and speed
- Add new features and customization options
- Fix bugs or issues you might experience
- Strengthen your phone's security to protect against threats

To check for updates:

- Go to **Settings > Software update > Download and install**

You can also allow automatic updates for apps through the **Play Store** by opening the **Play Store > Settings > Network preferences > Auto-update apps**.

Taking a few minutes to check for updates regularly can help you avoid bigger problems down the line.

Exploring More at Your Own Pace

This guide has taken you through the essentials of using your Samsung Galaxy S25 Ultra. But remember— there's always more to discover.

As you grow more comfortable:

- Try exploring features you haven't used yet, like **Bixby routines**, **digital stylus tools**, or **photo editing apps**.
- Join online forums or watch how-to videos at your convenience.
- Ask family members or friends to show you something new.

You don't have to master everything at once. Go step by step, revisit chapters when needed, and continue learning at your own pace.

Resources for Further Learning

If you want to go beyond this guide, here are a few reliable resources:

- **Samsung Members App** – Pre-installed on your phone. Offers tips, troubleshooting help, and official support.
- **Samsung.com** – Visit the Help section for user manuals and video tutorials.
- **YouTube Tutorials** – Many tech experts post step-by-step videos for Galaxy users.
- **Local Classes or Tech Help Centers** – Some community centers or libraries offer free phone training sessions.
- **Google Search** – When in doubt, typing a simple question like "How to use split-screen on Galaxy S25 Ultra" can lead to helpful results.

These options can help you gain more confidence and stay updated with new features.

Appendix

A. Glossary of Common Smartphone Terms

This glossary provides simple explanations of common smartphone-related terms to help you better understand your Galaxy S25 Ultra.

- **Wi-Fi** – A wireless internet connection used at home or in public places.
- **Bluetooth** – A wireless connection used to pair your phone with other devices like headphones or speakers.
- **GPS** – Global Positioning System; helps apps like Maps determine your location.
- **App** – A software program on your phone, like the Camera, Messages, or Calendar.
- **Cloud** – Online storage for saving photos, documents, or contacts.
- **Home Screen** – The main screen you see when you unlock your phone.

- **App Drawer** – A complete list of all apps installed on your phone.

- **Notification** – A message or alert that pops up to let you know something happened.

- **Settings** – The area where you control your phone's functions and features.

- **Touchscreen** – The surface of your phone that responds to taps, swipes, and gestures.

Understanding Icons and Status Symbols

Your phone's status bar (at the top of the screen) displays small icons. Here are a few common ones:

- **Wi-Fi symbol** – Shows you're connected to a wireless network.

- **Mobile signal bars** – Indicates the strength of your mobile service.

- **Battery icon** – Shows how much charge is left.

- **Bluetooth symbol** – Indicates Bluetooth is on and connected.

- **Alarm clock icon** – Shows an alarm is set.

- **Airplane mode icon** – Means all wireless connections are turned off.

Each icon helps you quickly understand your phone's current condition.

B. Quick Reference Charts

Navigation Gesture Cheat Sheet

Gesture	What It Does
Swipe up from bottom	Go to Home screen
Swipe up and hold	View recent apps
Swipe left or right from the edge	Go back
Double-tap screen	Turn screen on or off
Pinch in/out	Zoom in or out on screen content

Accessibility Features at a Glance

Feature	Function
Font Size	Makes text easier to read
High Contrast Mode	Improves text visibility
TalkBack	Reads screen content aloud
Magnifier Window	Enlarges parts of the screen
Assistant Menu	Adds a touch-friendly shortcut panel

Common App Icons and What They Mean

Icon	App
Phone	Make calls
Messages	Send texts

Gmail	Email access
Chrome	Internet browsing
Camera	Take photos and videos
Gallery	View saved photos
Maps	GPS and directions
Settings	Adjust phone preferences

C. Recommended Apps for Seniors

Here are helpful apps designed to be easy to use and practical for daily life:

Health, News, Entertainment, and Communication

- **Samsung Health** – Track steps, sleep, and more
- **Medisafe** – Pill reminder and medication tracking

- **BBC News or NPR News** – Trusted news with large text support
- **Spotify** – Listen to music, podcasts, or radio
- **YouTube** – Watch how-to videos, documentaries, or entertainment
- **Zoom** – Video calls with family and friends
- **WhatsApp** – Simple texting and calling with photo/video sharing

Apps with Senior-Friendly Interfaces

- **Big Launcher** – Enlarges text and icons for easier visibility
- **Simple Mode (Built-in)** – A built-in Samsung feature that simplifies your Home screen
- **Magnifying Glass + Flashlight** – A handy tool for reading small print
- **Google Assistant** – Use your voice to search, text, or ask questions
- **Bible or Prayer Apps** – Easy-to-read versions for spiritual inspiration

All of these apps can be found and downloaded through the **Google Play Store**.

D. Helpful Websites and Support Resources

Links to Official Samsung Help

- **Samsung Support Home:**
  www.samsung.com/support
- **Samsung Members App (Pre-installed):**
  Get device tips, live chat with support, and troubleshoot problems.
- **Find My Mobile:**
  findmymobile.samsung.com

How to Contact Customer Support

- **Samsung Phone Support (U.S.):**
  1-800-SAMSUNG (1-800-726-7864)
  Open Monday–Friday, 8 AM to 12 AM EST
- **Samsung Live Chat:**
  Available via the Samsung Members app or website.
- **In-Store Support:**
  Visit your nearest Samsung Experience Store or carrier store.